To

From

Bless This House

Bless This House

ANN WALL FRANK

ILLUSTRATIONS BY MARLENE K. GOODMAN

CB
CONTEMPORARY BOOKS
A TRIBUNE NEW MEDIA/EDUCATION COMPANY

Library of Congress Cataloging-in-Publication Data

Frank, Ann Wall.
    Bless this house : a collection of blessings to
make a house your home / Ann Wall Frank ;
illustrations by Marlene K. Goodman.
        p.   cm.
    Includes bibliographical references (p. 107).
    ISBN 0-8092-3197-2
    1. House blessings.   I. Title.
BL619.H68F73   1996
291.3'8—dc20   95-50300
                                        CIP

Published by Contemporary Books, Inc.
Two Prudential Plaza, Chicago, Illinois 60601-6790
Manufactured in the United States of America
International Standard Book Number: 0-8092-3197-2
10   9   8   7   6   5   4   3   2   1

For Jeff

Contents

Bless This House

Introduction

*M*ANY OF US, NOT JUST architects and artists, writers and poets, seers and shamans, know that a house has a soul. We can walk into a shabby bungalow, decorated in hand-me-downs so old they're chic again, and feel a warmth, a comfort, a love, that seems to radiate from every corner, enveloping us in safety, peace, and tranquility. Or we can enter a grand, flawlessly appointed mansion and sense a sad and gloomy energy that no amount of wealth or designer decor can conceal. Sooner or later, a house becomes an entity all its own.

And that entity is so much more than mere shelter. Home is, above all, a cluster of memories. We recall our childhood homes at the smell of fresh bread or the eccentric creak of an old oak floorboard. The cabbage roses on the attic wallpaper are still etched in our mind's eye. We smell lilac and drift back to a grandmother's garden.

When we are five and when we are ninety-five, we ache for home.

In almost every culture, home is the calm haven that sustains the spirit, the center where our affections, hopes, and dreams collect, the safe, welcoming place where we shelter our loved ones and nourish our souls. As the frenzy of the outside world encroaches on our psyches and on our bodies, home, more than ever, is where we find our hearts.

As long as there have been homes, there have been rites and rituals to bless, protect, and celebrate them. The seeds of many ancient rituals continue to flower, at least in part, in today's house blessings. One example is the housewarming. In prehistoric times the hearth fire symbolized the soul of the family. When the eldest son departed to begin his own family, he took a piece of the ancestral fire with him to keep that spirit alive from generation to generation. Today many of us still refer to the hearth as the "heart" of the home, and the first fire lit in a new dwelling is called a housewarming.

Rituals and blessings are as important as ever in helping us connect to the deeper meaning of our lives and

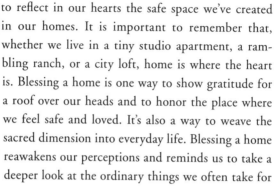

to reflect in our hearts the safe space we've created in our homes. It is important to remember that, whether we live in a tiny studio apartment, a rambling ranch, or a city loft, home is where the heart is. Blessing a home is one way to show gratitude for a roof over our heads and to honor the place where we feel safe and loved. It's also a way to weave the sacred dimension into everyday life. Blessing a home reawakens our perceptions and reminds us to take a deeper look at the ordinary things we often take for granted. Caring for our actual houses, however humble they are, writes Thomas Moore in *Care of the Soul,* is also care for *our* soul: "No matter how little money we have, we can be mindful of the importance of beauty in our homes. No matter where we live, we live in a neighborhood, and we can cultivate this wider piece of earth, too, as our home, as a place that is integrally bound to the condition of our hearts."

Grafting heart to home, as Thomas Moore suggests, doesn't have to be a formal ceremony or a religious ritual. It can be as humble as an inner commitment to harmony, as simple as placing fresh flowers on the table, as quiet as lighting a candle in the evening, or as personal as saying a prayer for protection. By filling our home with the symbols of our heart's desire, we can live more spiritually from day to day.

There are as many ways to bless a home as there are kinds of people to fill it. This book offers a glimpse of the traditions behind a few of the blessings, rituals, and folklore practiced around the world's homes. Each shows a unique *personality*—a joyful, magical, and ebullient quality, perhaps, or a quiet reverence for home and the souls who live there.

Some common threads and universal themes run through many of the blessings and rites in this book. One is the ritual feast, a sharing of the bounty of home with neighbors, family, and friends. Another is the concept of purifying our homes, making our spaces sacred, preparing them for our own spirit's habitation. Nearly every blessing commences with the acknowledgment of residual presences or spirits. These unseen inhabitants may be ceremoniously exorcised with passion and drama, or they may be simply, respectfully, and politely asked to leave.

The concept of renewal also unites the blessings of different cultures. Blessing a home is a kind of spring-cleaning for the soul. One of the best places to begin a spiritual, emotional, and physical renewal is within our own dwelling, because homes are the earthly templates for our spiritual life. We have a chance for extraordinary creativity and rejuvenation inside those four walls.

Through the course of making our way in today's hectic world, we can end up in a bracing clatter of everyday existence just to survive. Home, then, becomes a true sanctuary, whether we practice a formal religion or not. We make our homes sacred by loving them. We love our homes for the very reason poet and writer May Sarton said: "It is the place of renewal and of safety; where for a little while there will be no harm or attack and, while every sense is nourished, the soul rests."

May your home be so abundantly blessed.

1

Ho' Omaika'l l Ka Hale: An Old Hawaiian House Blessing

THE ANCIENT HAWAIIANS practiced a charming ceremony to consecrate their homes. The seeds of that ceremony have flowered in the Christian tradition of contemporary Hawaiian blessings.

The house was the most sacred possession of the early settlers of this island chain. The dwelling was not only their shelter, but the center where the family's *mana*, or spiritual forces, would develop over a lifetime. Protecting the good of the *mana*, along with thwarting negative influences, was so important to the Hawaiians that they built the fence before they built the house. The fence was a barrier to evil.

The early Hawaiian house was embraced as a living, breathing part of the universe, and like a newborn baby, it had its own ceremony for consecration, called the *piko* cutting. As a symbol that the house had been born into the world, the house builder left a small tuft of thatch, called the *piko*, hanging loose like an umbilical cord over the threshold. The morning of the house blessing ceremony, the family gathered greens and flowers from the forest as a sweet and fragrant invitation to the gods to join in the festivities. The Hawaiians involved the gods in every aspect of house building, from selecting the home site to preparing their favorite foods for the feast.

Once the house was completed, the *piko* was cut by the village Kahuna, who would pronounce the house free from the world and, with a prayer, graft it to its family. A common *piko*-cutting prayer follows:

> *O Kane, O Ku, O Lono,*
> *I am cutting the navel core of the house, O gods,*
> *A house to revive life,*
> *A house to extend life.*
> *Grant life to a sick man who enters this "house*
> *   of life,"*
> *A person who enters this* hale ola,
> *A person near death who enters this* hale ola.

Grant life (well-being) to me, your descendant in
    this world,
Grant life to my wife,
Grant life to my children,
Grant life to my siblings,
Grant life to my parents,
Grant life to my entire family.
May there be well-being in this
    earthly life.

'Amana; *the* kapu *of the prayer is freed.*

The *piko*-cutting ceremony was exclusive to the
Kahuna and the family; only their *mana*, or spirit, could
fill the house before the consecration. Afterward, others
could join in the festivities.

Once the *piko* was cut and the new threshold was in
place, the family brought the mats and furnishings inside
and filled the house with the fresh flowers and greens and
laid fresh ripe bananas on the lanai (porch) as an offering. Then the women opened the ovens, and a fabulous
feast of pig, chicken, and fish was prepared. While the

food cooked, the family placed a red fish (*Kumu* or *weke*), and a white fish (*'ama 'ama*) under the threshold or a central pillar to release luck into the house. After a prayer invoking the family's immediate ancestors to join in, the family and guests devoured the food. Custom dictated that not a crumb could remain in the house, and the bones had to be burned.

The celebration lasted for days. Gifts were opened and adored; jokes, anecdotes, and family stories revisited their endless incarnations; spontaneous hula dances and chants garnered rounds of applause. After the last of the prayers had been said, the *piko* had been cut, and the feast had been eaten, the home was considered to be consecrated. The family could safely set up housekeeping.

Today, when a new house is built, we can adopt this ancient Hawaiian blessing by leaving a board protruding to be nailed in or smoothed by a saw after a blessing is recited. Afterward, a feast may be shared with family and friends. When we move into a previously owned house, we can follow the Hawaiian tradition of sprinkling all the rooms and the outside of the house with salt or holy water using

ti leaves, saying, "The house stands, the house is solid."
When we have finished, we can recite a benediction such
as the following Hawaiian Daily House Prayer:

> *O my guardians, from remote antiquity,*
> *Watch over our home*
> *From top to bottom;*
> *From one corner to the other;*
> *From east to west;*
> *From the side facing the sea;*
> *From the inside to the outside,*
> *Watch over and protect it;*
> *Ward off all that may trouble our life here.*

> *Amana* (the prayer) *is freed.*

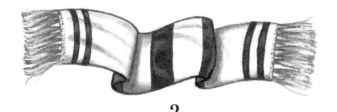

2

The Attaching of a Mezuzah

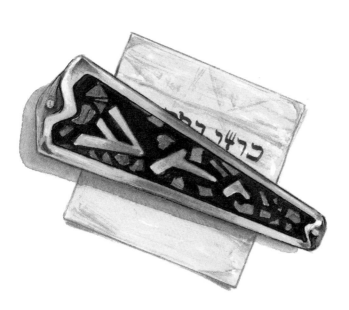

*T*HE JEWS HAVE BLESSINGS for everything under and including the sun—blessings on fruit, on hearing thunder, on receiving new clothes, on recovery from illness, on children, on meals with bread and on meals without bread, on morning, on seeing rainbows, on strawberries, on the sea. According to Jewish law, everything that God has created is good: food, sex, beautiful things. The Talmud says that we must account for missing or denying ourselves innocent pleasures. Life is neutral; people make it holy.

The Temple of Jerusalem, built by King Solomon, was an essential part of early Jewish faith and the place that housed the Ark of the Covenant, which held God's laws for man.

When the Temple was destroyed by the Romans in A.D. 70, after being rebuilt again and again, the house became the holy place for these fugitive souls. Today

some Jews leave a corner of the home empty and undec-
orated for *zeher lahurban*—the rememberance of the
destruction of the Temple.

A Jew cannot live at home alone; he or she
must have community, for we are all intercon-
nected. Abraham, the original dependable host, had a tent
with all four sides as doors, open to travelers and visitors.

Many Jews bring bread, candles, and salt to a new
home before moving in. The bread symbolizes the hope
that food will be abundant; the candles reflect the light
and joy that will pervade the home, and the salt is a
reminder of Leviticus 2:13, which says salt shall be a part
of all sacrificial worship.

The Torah commands that Jews sanctify their homes.
This is done, among other rituals, with the attaching of
the mezuzah. *Mezuzah*, meaning doorpost, refers to
Deuteronomy 6:9, 11:20, commanding the Jews to write
the essentials of their faith on the doorposts and the gates
of their houses. A true mezuzah is handwritten on parchment by a pious scribe. The container is a mere *objét*—it
could be wax paper for the significance it carries. The
home dweller inspects the parchment two times every

seven years to make sure it is still legible. If not, a new mezuzah must replace it.

Though the mezuzah is not intended as a talisman, folklore surrounds it. As early as Talmudic times, the mezuzah *did* become a mystic amulet to some Jews, who thought it would protect the house from evil spirits. One legend has it that in homes where someone has had a heart attack, the unrolled parchment will reveal a tiny hole through the word *heart.* Few Jews today think of a mezuzah as a protective amulet; far more regard the mezuzah as a reminder, when coming and going, that the affairs of the world are small things.

The dedication of the Jewish home is called *Hanukat Habayit.* While there is no established form for the ceremony, there is a Biblical reference to the dedication of a new house in Deuteronomy 20:5. The *Hanukat Habayit* can be as simple as reciting blessings for the home and fastening the mezuzah, singing, and meditating. Some families read from Psalm 15, which describes the Jewish ideal of human conduct. Before the mezuzah is attached, this blessing is said:

Blessed are You, Lord our God, King of the Universe,
who has sanctified us with your Commandments, commanding us to affix the mezuzah to the doorposts
of our homes.

Blessed are You, Lord our God, King of the
Universe, who has kept us alive and sustained us
and permitted us to reach this moment.

After the blessing, the mezuzah is attached to the
upper third of the right-hand side of the entry door, with
the top tilted toward the room being entered.

As a reminder of God's omniscience, many Jews kiss
their fingers and touch the mezuzah whenever they leave
and return to their home.

In October, some Jews honor the harvest festival of
Sukkot, an observance dating back to the Feast of Tabernacles when God commanded the Jews to build their
own tabernacles and live in them for seven days. For the
week of Sukkot, Jews live in the simplest, most temporal
shelter a human being could make; a flimsy and fragile
construction with a roof of greenery. It's here that they

sleep, pray, and eat. Sukkot is an annual reminder to the Jews that they are at the whim of the elements and completely in the hands of God. By observing Sukkot, Jews remember that home is necessary to life, but not sufficient for the spirit.

3

Kat' Íkon Ekklisía: A Greek Orthodox House Blessing

A CONCERN FOR CONTINUITY and tradition characterizes the Orthodox branch of Christianity. In Orthodox Christianity, the blithe currents of everyday life are made sacred by feasts and fasts, by celebrations for Easter eggs, by baking of communion bread, by blessing a new baby, by blessing a new house.

To the Orthodox Greeks, the home is literally a little church, for the church is composed not only of bishops or of clergy, but of the whole laity. The term *kat' íkon ekklisía*, when it was coined by Saint Paul in the first century, referred to the gathering of Christians in private homes before there were churches. Today it refers to the spiritual atmosphere the Orthodox create in their homes by following the rich traditions of their faith.

House blessings are typically performed by a priest before the family moves into the home and at the annual feast of Epiphany, honoring the baptism of Christ in the

River Jordan and the worship of the holy Trinity. Epiphany is celebrated on January 6.

The use of basil in a Greek Orthodox house blessing is attributed to Saint Helena, the mother of Constantine the Great. When in her eighties, Saint Helena had a vision of where Christ's crucifixion cross was buried. Helena made a pilgrimage to the Holy Land, found the fragrant, basil-covered hill of her vision in Jerusalem, and dug. She unearthed the nails of the crucifixion and the seamless coat Christ wore on his journey. Today, basil is dipped in holy water and sprinkled around the house by the priest.

Olive oil is also part of the blessing, a symbol alluding to the Biblical account of the Great Flood. When the rain stopped, Noah (Genesis 8:11) sent a dove to search for dry land. The bird returned with an olive branch, a symbol of God's love and promise for the future. A lamp of burning oil graces Orthodox blessings today.

Along with basil and olive oil, the icon altar, or *ikonostási*, is an important part of the Orthodox house blessing. Orthodox icons are unparalleled in any other Christian tradition, and almost every religious Greek Orthodox household has an elaborate *ikonostási*. The *ikonostási* holds religious art and images of saints for whom family members are named. Saints reveal the myriad qualities of the personal God; they are windows to heaven. Icons are the windows to the windows.

In addition to the icons, the altar holds candles, burning oil (or a lamp), incense, and a bowl of water, which symbolizes purification, bodily health, and life-creating spirit.

One of the deep joys of Orthodox worship is the wealth of hymns created during the Byzantine Middle Ages to mark the various liturgical cycles. During the house blessing the priest immerses a crucifix in holy water and sprinkles all the members of the family, the icon altar, and the rooms of the house, chanting the hymns and prayers of the Orthodox as he does so. The following excerpt is part of a prayer for the blessing of a home that has not been blessed before:

O God, our Savior, who was pleased to enter under the roof of Zacchaeus, thereby bringing salvation to him and to all his household: Protect from every injury those who have chosen to live in this house and who address their prayers and petitions to you through us your unworthy servants; keep them safe from all harm; bless this their dwelling and preserve their lives unassailable.

The priest then asks that abundant and divine grace enter the home. The priest prays that the family be filled with the sanctification of God through the drinking and sprinkling of the water, and that it bring health to body and soul. Families keep extra vials of the holy water in the medicine cabinet to sip as a spiritual and physical elixir throughout the year.

4

The Zuni and Sha-La-K' O

ZUNI PUEBLO LIES in the valley of a tiny tributary of the Colorado River, high in an ancient desert of western New Mexico, nearly touching the Arizona border. In the early 1530s a Franciscan missionary visited the village, known to its ancient inhabitants as *Halona I 'tiwana*, the Middle Ant Hill of the World. Stories of fabulous wealth and splendor floated back to Spanish rulers of Mexico, and in 1540, Francisco Vásquez de Coronado led an expedition of conquest. The spoils were exaggerated, but the conquerors succeeded in bringing the Zuni people under Spanish—and Franciscan—rule. They failed, however, to supplant Zuni religion with their own.

The Zunis' vast creation mythology tells that the location of their village was set by a water spider, an insect that stretched its body across the continent with its heart resting at Zuni. This is the Zuni Middle Place, the sacred ground between the sacred compass, or four directions and their corresponding animal totems, and between zenith (that which is above) and nadir (that which is below). Through their elaborate and ancient ceremonial lore, Zunis practice the oldest religion in the Western Hemisphere. Rich in cosmology, ripe with ritual, and pulsating with symbolic ceremony, the Zuni religion permeates every detail of ordinary existence. For Zunis, religion *is* life, and ritual magic transforms everyday objects—corn and cornmeal, pollen, tobacco, stones and shells, feathers and masks—into sacred fetishes and offerings.

The Zuni house is a microcosm; the village is at once a particular place and the entire universe. The interweaving of activity fans out from the center of the individual homes, which are owned by women. Pueblo society is matrilineal.

One of the most dramatic ceremonies is the annual *Sha-la-k' o* observance, enacted each year around the winter equinox, when the gods, or kachinas, return to earth. *Sha-la-k' o* is a hunt ceremony, a ceremony consecrating new homes and a spiritual renewal for the pueblo.

Innumerable variations of the ceremony exist from town to town and from tribe to tribe, but *Sha-la-k' o* always delivers drama. Once the Zuni tribal principals select the organizers and impersonators of the gods for *Sha-la-k' o*, an arduous daily rehearsal begins. By October the pace is frenetic, and the impersonators, also called kachinas, receive a string tied with forty-nine knots, one to be ceremoniously untied each morning until the festival's end. Special rooms have been built for the gods in the pueblo houses, usually the new ones that have been chosen for dedication. The houses are decorated for the gods in brilliant colors and elaborate attire.

A great bull roar and a deep hammering Paleolithic sound reverberates through the pueblo, announcing the beginning of *Sha-la-k' o*. The gods descend on the pueblo in their ingeniously made, other-worldly effigies. They may be bulge-eyed, horn-snouted, or nearly nude with long-snouted red masks, wearing a collar of crow feathers and deep green helmets. Figures twelve feet high with massive heads, shocks of long black hair, and long, square-ended wooden beaks like raging demon birds arrive in their glory. Among them are a high priest, a priest of the sun, and a fire god, who gradually cross the river and make their way toward the pueblo as the chanting builds. The tension mounts to an almost frenetic level, and the holy Fools—towering, masked, painted joking performers of satire—provide comic relief. Ceremony, dancing, and celebration continue for days, often with ritual possession.

On the eighth day, masked *Sha-la-k' o* impersonators and kachina dancers are guided by priests to a new house, where prayers and ceremonials are said before the ladders of the houses to be entered. The priests descend through the sky hole and crouch near the side of an altar, where immense fires of pungent piñon wood burn. They pray, they chant, they clap their huge beaks and roll their bobbing eyes to the music, or contort and gyrate at signals from the singers and drummers, their head plumes brushing the rafters. Homeowners offer them a feast. They eat, dance, sing, and drink all night.

Just as the morning star rises, the music dies, and the chief dancer is led to the center of the room and elaborately costumed. The priest of the sun takes the dancer up the ladder to the roof, where they chant a prayer to the waning sun of the old year. At dawn, the impersonators are washed, fed, plied with gifts. Then they return to their own homes, signifying the culmination of this incredible religious spectacle.

5

Feng Shui: At Home with the Chinese Dragon

*F*ENG SHUI (which means, literally, the wind and the water), is not really a house blessing, but the art of placing and orienting objects in concert with the environment to bring mental, spiritual, financial, and physical well-being. *Feng shui* is a package of folklore that combines metaphysics, astrology, intuition, and environmental and cultural doctrine with roots in Taoist philosophy and the I Ching.

Feng shui is based in part on *chi*, positive energy or cosmic breath, and *sha*, or killing dagger, the straightlined and negative force. According to the laws of *feng shui*, if you change your environment, you can change the energy around you, and thereby change your life.

Feng shui is a serious and honorable practice that often takes generations to master. There are dozens of books on *feng shui* and its different schools, from the works of Taoist masters to westernized primers for the beginner. The following principles are just a few of the most basic.

The ideal house rests in an "armchair," that is, a site like a nest with a hill rising behind the structure and smaller hills on each side. The hill represents the Chinese dragon, an awesome, bountiful, and imperious force—it's best to be in its lap. If the property slopes down in the front and if you have a view of mountains or water, luck is yours. Water, flowing or circulating nearby, around, or through a site brings prosperity.

Chi is round, soft, quiet, balanced, and feminine. *Chi* needs a clear path to undulate through the universe, your body, and your house. *Chi* needs balance. Too much glass, for instance, causes *chi* to flood the house, resulting in tension. *Chi* travels the earth's magnetic fields, which run from north to south. Ideally, the entrance and exits of a home should be off center; if they are directly lined up, the *chi* rushes through the house too quickly, gathering too much energy in its wake. A wind chime or crystal hung in its path will balance the *chi* in the room.

Ideal *feng shui* balances each of these elements:

- Wood—A treed site is good, but not always possible. Protect the house by planting a tree in the northwest corner. Decorate the interior of the house with plants that have rounded leaves (to reflect *chi*), bamboo, rectangular shapes (which represent wood), and the color green.
- Fire—Fire is represented in pointed and sharp shapes (like the flames of a fire), human and animal life, pictures of animals, plants with pointed leaves, fireplaces, wood stoves, candles, and the colors red, rose, and pink.
- Earth—Earth elements come from dirt, sand, marble, tile, stone, and the colors yellow, green, and brown.
- Metal—Metal is represented in objects made of gold, silver, brass, and even tinfoil.
- Water—Water is represented by an aquarium, a bowl of clean water, a fountain, and the colors black, indigo blue, forest green, and "clear" (as in plastic and glass).

According to the principles of *feng shui*, abundance will come if you create a wealth corner diagonally opposite the primary entrance to your home. A living plant (with round leaves) placed there will boost health and energy. Place a copper bowl (copper is the color of wealth) in the corner and add coins, family photos, or a symbol of health such as a picture of nature.

Invest in a fish pond. Aquariums and fish ponds are standard fixtures in Chinese restaurants, for good reason. The word *fish* sounds like the word *abundance* in Chinese, and fish are auspicious creatures. Place an odd number of fish (odd numbers represent yang, the stronger male energy) in a clean pond or aquarium. Two of the fish should be darker than the others to absorb any negative energy in the dwelling.

And fix dripping faucets. Leaky faucets can mean letting your resources drip away.

Painting the front door red will encourage good luck. A wind chime hung just inside the door will promote mental, emotional, and spiritual clarity.

To keep unwanted forces from entering while you sleep, place your bed where you can easily see the door. A round mirror in the bedroom will bring peace of mind, but do not place it over the bed. According to *feng shui*, your spirit travels at night while you sleep. Don't make it bounce off the mirror back into your body. You can wake up with bruises.

For insight, place books where you can see them when you enter the front door.

Sha is known as the death arrow in *feng shui*. *Sha* travels in a straight line, collecting in hospitals, cemeteries, stagnant water, power lines, neon signs, or any thing, place, or sound that "pierces" your home. Fortunately, *feng shui* has an antidote. In many places in the Far East, as well as in American Chinatowns, eight-sided mirrors called *ba guas* are a fixture on the outside of homes and businesses. These mirrors deflect *sha*, sending the negative vibrations back to their source.

6

A Traditional Balinese House Blessing

BALI IS AN EXOTIC, mysterious, and magical land, pulsating with the struggle to maintain balance between the dueling forces of good and evil. Balinese Hinduism is earthy and animistic and steeped in ceremony. To say the Balinese have rituals for their houses is like saying there is a little greenery in a rain forest. Bali *is* ritual. Elaborate ceremonies link the Balinese with every aspect of their existence, including building a house.

The traditional Balinese house, or *bale*, models the universe and *becomes* a part of the universe when it is consecrated. Where and how to build is guided by the old village laws, or *adat*. Construction requires a team of knowledgeable architects and builders to interpret and execute these laws. No wise person would dream of beginning to design or construct a home before investigating the spirits in the ground to be dug, in the trees to be felled, in the rocks to be moved. Spirits dwell in all these things, and apologies for their relocation are as important as the floor plan. In the same vein, choosing an auspicious day to begin construction is critical; to do otherwise invites an ambush of evil spirits.

The Balinese house is modeled after a human body. The head is the roof, the body and pillars the support, the feet the foundation. When a site for the family compound has been selected, the architect, or *undagi*, measures important body parts of the eldest male in the family, such as the width of his index finger and the width of his palm. These measurements become the template for the house layout and size.

The communal family temple is the most sacred part of the house and is built first. The temple or shrine is oriented *kaja*, or toward the sacred mountains and homes of the gods. *Kaja* is the east corner of the compound. Family members sleep with their heads—their most sacred body part—*kaja*, while the animals are kept *kelod*, or away from the mountains.

Families in Bali have their own family gods. The household temple is where the family prays to these gods and where they worship the purified and deified souls of their ancestors. Almost all household temples have a *sanggah*, *pemerajan*, or shrine of origin, which is divided into three side-by-side sections. One represents the male ancestral group, one the female ancestral group, and one the sun or the sun god.

When a young Balinese couple marry, a new shrine is erected in the family compound. At first it is flimsy, made of bamboo resting on four live trunks. When the marriage proves to be durable, a new permanent shrine replaces the first. It is standard to erect an offering column in the house for the *ngurah* or *ngerurah*, the protector of the ground, and a column for the *taksu*, the intercessor between gods and people.

A village priest performs the house inauguration ceremony, which is called *melaspasin*. The priest says prayers over each part of the house and buries offerings to the

gods at strategic locations to protect
the family from evil.

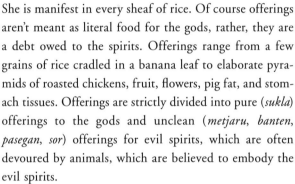

Rice offerings are common. Sri
Dewi, the goddess of maturing rice, is
also the wife of Sedana, the god of wealth.
She is manifest in every sheaf of rice. Of course offerings
aren't meant as literal food for the gods, rather, they are
a debt owed to the spirits. Offerings range from a few
grains of rice cradled in a banana leaf to elaborate pyra-
mids of roasted chickens, fruit, flowers, pig fat, and stom-
ach tissues. Offerings are strictly divided into pure (*sukla*)
offerings to the gods and unclean (*metjaru, banten,
pasegan, sor*) offerings for evil spirits, which are often
devoured by animals, which are believed to embody the
evil spirits.

When the house is completed, the Balinese dress the
house with clothes that correspond to people. The eaves
are decorated with long strips of cloth like hair, and a
head cloth is wrapped around the top of each pillar. The
house "clothes" change with the varying celebrations.

7

Hogan Biyin: A Navajo Blessing

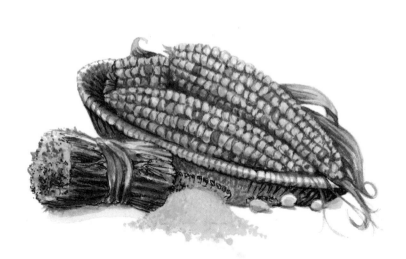

*L*and is the Navajo church. Restoring harmony between humanity and earth is the thrust of the Navajo spiritual tradition. The laws of nature require the Navajos to conduct themselves wisely with the Holy People. When they live in harmony with the land, nobody fights.

Navajo religion, dogma, practice, and ritual are fantastically complex. Ceremonial lore is extremely important and includes every conceivable aspect of nature, deity, culture, imagination, behavior, emotion, and supernatural power. Everything in the universe—material and abstract—is perceived through its effect on people. If a person knows about something and can control it through ritual and ceremony, it is good. If not, it is evil.

Ceremonial fetishes, offerings, songs, and prayers play a crucial role in Navajo ritual. Prayer sticks, masks, body paint, herbs and plants, pollen (the essence of life), wands, hoops, feathers and beads are a fraction of the ceremonial tools used in rituals.

The Hogan Blessing seeks good fortune for the hogan (the dwelling in which a family takes shelter), the family, and the tribe and protection from evil. The first Navajo hogans to receive this blessing were crude brush shelters, built round to strike harmony with the circle of sky and to mirror the great domed canopy of heaven above. By the eighteenth century the hogan had become a substantial dwelling, made of logs chinked with mud and moss and sometimes completely covered with earth. Some hogans were made of adobe bricks and stones. Today, most hogans are hexagonal log homes with domed roofs.

The hogan represents deity, and the door of the hogan always faces east, toward the rising sun. The fireplace, or altar, is in the center. It represents the hogan's cosmic center. The smoke from the fire curls up through a hole in the ceiling so that the smell of the incense can reach the nostrils of the gods.

Around the turn of the century, traditional Navajo Hogan Blessings took place at the culmination of the building of the dwelling. When the hogan was ready for dedication, the wife swept the floor and lit a fire under the smoke hole. Then she poured cornmeal into a shallow basket for her husband, the head of the family, who rubbed the dry meal on the timbers of the hogan as a gift to the gods. As the husband sprinkled the meal around the perimeter of the floor, he prayed:

> *May it be delightful, my house;*
> *From my head, may it be delightful;*
> *To my feet, may it be delightful;*
> *Where I lie, may it be delightful;*
> *All above me, may it be delightful;*
> *All around me, may it be delightful.*

He then tossed meal into the fire, saying:

> *May it be delightful and well, my fire.*

He tossed cornmeal up through the smoke hole, saying:

May it be delightful, Sun, my mother's ancestor,
*   for this gift;*
May it be delightful, as I walk around my house.

The husband continued the chant as he sprinkled meal
outside the doorway:

May it be delightful this road of
*   light, my mother's ancestor.*

His wife then made her offering of meal to the fire:

May it be delightful, my fire;
May it be delightful for my children; may all be
*   well;*
May it be delightful with my food and theirs;
*   may all be well;*
All my possessions, well may they be made to
*   increase;*
All my flocks, well may they be made to increase.

This ceremony was followed by a house welcoming party with friends and family, who ate, smoked, and told stories.

After an interval of a few days, the formal house devotions and blessings were observed. These rites were presided over by a devotional singer or shaman, carefully selected for the beauty of his songs.

The devotional singer started the song, listening closely to hear whether the men of the tribe sang the correct words. Any omission or incorrect rendering would wreak havoc on the house and its dwellers. They sang devotional songs, which praised the delightful home, the corn, and the ancients, to each of the cardinal directions. After each repetition they sang this chant:

Before me, may it be delightful;
Behind me, may it be delightful;
Around me, may it be delightful;
Below me, may it be delightful;
Above me, may it be delightful;
All, may it be delightful.

When they had sung all of the songs of praise to the gods, they chanted prayers to the malign and evil influences, beseeching them not to come near the dwelling.

Contemporary Navajo houses and hogans are still considered to be sacred dwellings and are blessed with variations of the traditional ways.

8

The Shaker Benediction: Cleaning as Blessing

AY THE WORD *Shaker*, and many people think of furniture: Shaker chairs, Shaker rockers, Shaker tables, Shaker brooms, baskets, baking tins. The strict simplicity and no-frills functionalism of Shaker design has achieved an image of classic beauty that represents the best in American craft.

The Shakers' spiritual image has been thinned by a culture obsessed with decor, but what the Shakers made was not about interior design. The Shakers shaped their spirit into form as repeatedly and reliably as any Buddhist uttering a mantra. Their strivings for holiness were literally handiwork; by their labors to create a perfect craft, the world around them would be made perfect. To dedicate their hearts to God, the Shakers put their hands to work, for work was the religion of this mystical, communal, and fiercely celibate sect. (And back then, nobody liked their furniture but the Shakers themselves.)

"Shakers" was the name given to the United Society of Believers in Christ's Second Coming, in about 1750 in Great Britain, where it originated. Group leadership was organized in America, chiefly in upstate New York, by Mother Ann Lee, an illiterate but sensitive and religious woman who sought to create heaven on earth as dictated by her frequent visions. Her followers viewed her as Christ embodied in the female line. Not only was she a religious visionary, she had the gift of tongues, she could discern spirits, and she could create miracles.

The Shakers lived communally. Men and women were absolute equals, and all property was shared. Work was worship. The Millennial Laws, rules received by divine revelation in 1821, maintained order and told the Shakers the right way to do things, from the way they prayed to the color they painted the trim on their buildings to the way they made their furniture: precise, exact, and along the path of the straight and narrow, a favorite Shaker metaphor.

Quiet, simple, and spare, a Shaker house makes clear statements of spiritual intentions. The same aesthetic holds for the meetinghouses, where the few remaining Shakers spend most of their time, working, praying, and dancing.

According to Shaker belief, piety prospers in the well-scrubbed home and the well-scrubbed soul. Mother Ann told her followers, "Be neat and clean, for no unclean thing can enter heaven," and, "Clean your rooms well, for good spirits will not live where there is dirt. There is no dirt in heaven." Followers took her seriously.

Some Shaker hymns make sweeping the house a metaphor for sweeping clean the soul. "The Hancock Sweeping Gift" (1843) is a Shaker vision that Mother Ann Lee gave to a follower as a way to convey the Lord's command to "sweep clean" the floor of the heart.

Shaker history tells of a band of sisters who were handed a cup of gospel fire by Mother Ann's six messengers. Immediately overcome with the quickening power of shaking, the Elder Sister channeled these words: "I want nothing left in me that God disowns, and sisters do not do this work by the halves, but *be thorough and make our dwellings clean.*" The band of sisters marched off to the dairy house, where each received a broom from Mother, with these instructions: "Sweep the floors clean."

Sweeping the house was a sacred act, as reflected in this hymn by Sister Elizabeth Potter in 1839:

> *Sweep, sweep and cleanse your floor*
> *Mother's standing at the door. . . .*

Another hymn required a strong back and a strong spirit:

> *Bow down low, bow down low,*
> *Wash, wash, clean, clean, clean, clean,*
> *   scour and scrub,*
> *Scour and scrub from this floor*
> *The stains of sin.*

9

Old Basque Farmhouse Rituals

THE BEAUTIFUL BASQUE pastoral valley in north central Spain and in the Pyrénées-Atlantiques region of southwest France is remote and romantic. The Basques' ancient language, independent spirit, ironic wit, and love of freedom distinguish them from other Europeans. In the United States, most Basques are centralized in Nevada, Idaho, Wyoming, and California and keep their culture alive through a strong sense of social community, work, and the church.

Today Basques are almost exclusively devout Roman Catholics, proud of their patron saints Saint Ignatius of Loyola, the founder of the Jesuit Order, and Saint Francis Xavier. But Basques were converted to Christianity very late. Cut off geographically from other cultures, they developed a vast collection of myths and practices.

In ancient times the Basque house was a temple and a refuge protected by pagan rituals. Basques hung signs

and amulets on their houses to protect them:
stone crosses on the roof ridges, wooden
crosses nailed to the doors, crosses
painted in lime around the windows,
and crosses carved into the beams and lin-
tels. Amulets containing herbs, laurel, ashes, holy
bread, and other organics protected the householder from
the evil eye. When someone died in the house, a family
member took a tile from the roof to release his or her
soul. After the funeral, the stuffing of the dead person's
mattress was burned at the nearest crossroads. Plants and
bushes were considered to be protective, too. The family
put laurel branches on the roof of the farmhouse the
moment it was completed. Thistles drove away evil spirits.

In the rural Basque culture, the farmhouse contin-
ues as an entity unto itself. The family belongs to the
house. In European Basque communities, the house has
a name and its own family tomb in the cemetery. The
house is named for its first master, or the first male head
of the household, beginning with the first couple to make
it their home. When a man leaves his natal house to
marry, he takes on the name of his new house. The house

may burn down or collapse, but once it has been named, it exists as long as someone in the community remembers it and as long as its tomb remains in the cemetery.

The tradition of taking on the name of the house instead of a surname is preserved generation after generation. The lintel inscriptions announce the family name, the date the house was founded, and sometimes an offer of hospitality, as in this lintel inscription at Ibarrolle:

To friends first of all,
To the poor when they come,
To enemies, for who is without them?
To all I am open wide.

The door lintel and the tombstone of a house are strongly connected. Both are thresholds, and both reflect the Basques' respect for their ancestors and their community. The lintel announces the founders of the house and identifies its family; the tombstone announces the resting place of countless generations. House and tomb are so inseparable that if the house is sold, the deathstone goes with it.

The female head of household is responsible for the spiritual welfare of all the souls who have belonged to her house since its founding. In the Old Country, she prays for them at the tomb every Sunday before Mass and on holy days. In some rural French Basque communities, fresh laurel is blessed by the priest on Palm Sunday. The housewife then takes it home and divides it into small bunches, attaching newly blessed sprigs to crucifixes. She stores the remaining boughs in a cupboard. During the year she will burn them to calm storms and quell crises within the home.

Basque priests still make house calls to bless the homes of the congregation, sprinkling holy water in all the rooms and reciting and singing many of the blessings in the Basque language to keep part of the "Old Religion" alive. Various Catholic blessings are typically used to bless a modern Basque home. The priest goes from room to room, offering prayers for each area of the home, such as this blessing for the kitchen:

*O God, you fill the hungry with good
things.
Send your blessing on us, as we work in
this kitchen,
And make us ever thankful for our daily
bread.
Grant this through Christ our Lord.*

When the entire house has been blessed,
each person kisses a cross or holy icon,
which then is set in a place of honor. Everyone recites the Lord's Prayer.

Hospitality is such a deep part of the Basque culture
that brotherhood and sisterhood and a broad sense of
community is a sacred aspect of life. That is why, in so
many Basque homes, you'll see this plaque on the wall:

*Those who enter my home
Are in their home*

Home is still the Basque refuge, and many Basques
bless the house each time they come and go.

10

Irish House Blessings

*T*HE IRISH CAN MAKE almost any occasion merry—
a wake, a wedding, the birth of a baby, a saint's
birthday, the opening of a new pub, the blessing of a new
house. Irish humor is ripe, their hospitality is legendary.
The same people who have written pious blessings for the
home have given us this:

> *May the roof of your house never fall in,*
> *And those under it never fall out.*

From the Celtic traditions, which invested them with
an obstinate superstition, to Christianity, which revealed
God's hand in everything around them, the Irish delight
in ceremony. The Irish religious background is mixed
and enigmatic. Myth and history, fables and facts, are
practical partners. In primitive Ireland, the gods and
demigods thrive. The great Jove of the Celts was the

Dagda, or the Good Father. This imperious sun god ruled the weather and the crops; he was huge and loved feasts; he was wise and tireless. He could take the shape of a bird or a horse or a serpent. He could wreak havoc on anyone and anything. He was the source of all wisdom.

Saint Patrick had to rage and thunder against the Dagda and the sun worship and threaten all kinds of wrath to graft Christianity to pagan rites. The Irish Druids were so devoted to their sun god that Saint Patrick had to affix a pagan sun to the crucifix to get them to accept the new symbol and, ultimately, Christianity. But Saint Patrick's spiritual powers were phenomenal. He drove the serpents out of Ireland with a staff given to him by Jesus, and he used a shamrock to demonstrate the mystery of the Trinity to a pagan king. Christianity took hold in Ireland, but not without catching a few pagan beliefs in the net.

Contemporary Ireland is a Roman Catholic country, devoted to God as the creator of livelihood and life itself. Still, the old folklore and ancient mythology seep through some of the people's most pious practices. There is lust for heaven, fear of hell, and a pagan joy underneath it all. The Celts never formulated a religion as much as they stimulated the Irish imagination, and there is a delightful sense of dualism floating through the Irish world. There may be an overlay of pious Christian morality, daily prayers, and strict observance of holy days, but there's also a leprechaun in the wine cellar, helping himself to the best bottle.

The kitchen and the hearth are the core of the Irish house. In the Old Country, the peat fire still burns day and night throughout the year, a symbol of family continuity and hospitality toward visitors. In earlier times the fire dispelled evil spirits and warmed the milk of the dairy cow who shared the family home. It was thought that if the fire went out, the soul of the family went with it. The fire was, and still is, one of the most important religious symbols of the Irish home.

Today many Irish families still bless the home and
the fire each time a fire is built. This traditional Irish
house blessing is called Banking the Fire:

> *I preserve this fire as Christ has preserved*
>   *everyone.*
> *Mary on the roof ridge, Brigid in the middle,*
> *And the eight most powerful angels in the City of*
>   *Grace*
> *Protect this house and this hearth*
>   *and safeguard its people.*
> *Let us bank this fire in honour of Holy Patrick.*
> *May our house not be burnt or our people*
>   *murdered,*
> *And may the bright sun of tomorrow shine*
>   *on us all, at home or abroad.*

11

Create Your Own House Blessing

$\mathcal{S}$OME OF US WERE MEANT to create our own rituals. Maybe our circle of family and friends embraces more than a single ethnic or religious tradition, or perhaps we feel hypocritical or shallow dipping into religion just to ask that the dead bolts always work. But for new home dwellers who have a spiritual craving, just shampooing the carpet and signing a lease or a mortgage agreement seems sadly insufficient.

The most powerful and satisfying home blessings don't need elaborate rituals. The ideas in this chapter show how simple a blessing can be. These practices, combined or used alone, can be a satisfying dedication to a new home or a blessing for an old one in need of spiritual rejuvenation.

The following are some suggestions to create your own house blessing.

Smudge the house. Many cultures use this form of purification to cleanse spaces of old energy. Smudging, censing, or purifying with smoke comes from native peoples in both North and South America and dates back to pre-Columbian cultures. This practice uses smudge sticks—bundles of dried herbs such as sage, cedar, sweetgrass, juniper, and copal, lit and used as a purifying incense throughout the house. Precise directions for using the smudge are available in Native American literature, but many people use the smudge intuitively, trusting that the healing power of the herbs and the purifying energy of the smoke are cleansing the home.

Create an altar. Altars are a reference point for the spirit. Any surface can be an altar: a table, desk, mantel, trunk, bookshelf, nightstand, bathtub ledge. Create your own icons and you create metaphors for your deepest values: photos, family keepsakes, candles, incense, books, fresh flowers, music boxes, stones, even a tomato ripening on the windowsill—all are food for the soul.

Create a sacred space. Set aside a quiet spot that is to be used only for meditating, daydreaming, or looking out onto nature. Thomas Merton, the Trappist monk, said, "There should be at least a room or some corner where no one will find you and disturb you or notice you."

Combine candle and prayer affirmations. Saying an affirmation for each room of the house gives the home a spiritual identity. Start the blessing by giving every dweller an unused white candle in a glass or other safe candleholder. Begin outside the front door and say, "Bless this house. Keep it safe, sound, and full of love." After everyone is inside, proceed to each room, gather, and affirm a prayer or idea for each space.

Make a time capsule. Burying a time capsule containing a date, a message, a wish, or a prayer in the foundation of a new house plants poetry in the cells of a home. Create a poem or letter, or copy a favorite verse, psalm, or poem to enclose in the capsule as well.

Plant a tree for an ancestor. Plant one for every loved one you have room for, and name them accordingly.

Hold a housewarming. Invite friends, family, and anybody who had a part in making the house happen (even those you stopped speaking to), and enjoy an evening of food, drink, and friendship. Ask your guests to bring a can of food and leave it on the front porch. When the party is over, you can gather up the food and give it to a local homeless shelter.

Play your favorite music. Better, ask musical friends to bring their instruments and sing and play songs to usher out any remaining spirits.

12

Fifty Ways to Make a House Your Home

A HOUSE ISN'T A HOME until we fill it with our spirit and lock it into our hearts with love. As we settle into our new space, our spirit grows, filling it with our own creative gestures and our own special things. It takes a while for a house to transform itself from four walls and a roof to that place of peaceful refuge you ache for when you're away. With houses, as with most things, God dwells in the details. These simple things can help to make a house a home.

∽ 1 ∾

Keep fresh flowers in the house.

∽ 2 ∾

Plant an herb garden in the kitchen.

⤳ 3 ⤶

Leave a corner of your garden untended,
for the spirits to grow wild.

⤳ 4 ⤶

Create a "listening garden," by planting
ornamental grasses such as silver feather, ribbon grass,
or feather reed grass. It takes only a gentle breeze
to start their music.

⤳ 5 ⤶

Place salt (a purifier) on the thresholds of the doors.

⤳ 6 ⤶

Remove your shoes before you enter your home.
Leave the stress (and the dust) of the rest of
the world outside.

⤳ 7 ⤶

Burn cedar (a natural insect repellant) in the fireplace.

✌ 8 ✌

Keep a candle burning wherever you are in the house.

✌ 9 ✌

Collect something: salt and pepper shakers,
candlesticks, angels, demitasse cups.

✌ 10 ✌

Make an altar of candles in the bedroom.

✌ 11 ✌

Say a prayer before each meal.

✌ 12 ✌

Be aware of which window follows the sunrise and
sunset. Always keep it clean.

✌ 13 ✌

Set up an aquarium.

✌ 14 ✌

Place a Victorian gazing globe in the garden.

❧ 15 ❧

Have your priest, minister, rabbi, or shaman
officially bless the house.

❧ 16 ❧

Care for a plant, dog, cat, guinea pig, or fish.

❧ 17 ❧

Clean your oven.

❧ 18 ❧

Keep books in every room.

❧ 19 ❧

Put a gargoyle, angel, or other protective creature
in the garden.

❧ 20 ❧

Wash the threshold with salt and water.

❧ 21 ❧

Have your neighbors over for coffee.

~ 22 ~

Hang wind chimes outside.

~ 23 ~

Hang a bird feeder.

~ 24 ~

Save a branch of your Christmas tree and use it to
start the New Year's fire.

~ 25 ~

Hang verses of poems, haiku, or blessings written on
rice paper from trees in your yard.

~ 26 ~

Every year make a ritual meal around the first yield
from your fruit, vegetable, or herb garden.

~ 27 ~

Write a list of the comforts you want your home
to provide family and friends. Frame it and hang it
in the kitchen or family room.

❧ 28 ❧
Create a shrine for ancestral photos.

❧ 29 ❧
When you sweep your floors, imagine you are
sweeping away any stress or sadness in the house.
Throw the dust in the fireplace and burn it.

❧ 30 ❧
Hang a horseshoe over the front door.

❧ 31 ❧
Float fresh flowers in a bowl of clean water.

❧ 32 ❧
Purify the air with aromatic oils sprayed through a
mister.

❧ 33 ❧
Burn herbs and other fragrant plants such as
sage or myrrh.

❧ 34 ❧

Play music at the same time every day.

❧ 35 ❧

Clean out your cupboards. Give all canned food
to a homeless shelter.

❧ 36 ❧

If you build a house or are adding a fireplace,
put a family keystone in the surround. A keystone
can be any tile with your initials, special symbols,
or family crest.

❧ 37 ❧

Become a designated neighborhood
"safe house" for kids.

❧ 38 ❧

Write down your best recipes and pass them on
to a family member.

❧ 39 ❧

Fill your kitchen with the aroma of
freshly baked bread.

❧ 40 ❧

Put a clay or wood chicken or rooster in the kitchen,
which symbolizes good luck in European folklore.

❧ 41 ❧

Put a birdbath in the garden.

❧ 42 ❧

Cut fresh greens after a rain and bring them inside.
Put them in a bowl on the dinner table.

❧ 43 ❧

Open fresh organic soap and put it in a
bedroom or bath.

❧ 44 ❧

Plant thyme as a ground cover in dirt pathways or
between stepping stones. Every time you walk on it,
you release the fragrance.

~ 45 ~

Buy fragrant water such as gardenia or rose water, and
shake it lightly on the sheets when you make up a
fresh bed.

~ 46 ~

Choose doorbells, phones, and alarm clocks with the
most pleasing sounds.

~ 47 ~

Put all overhead lights (except the bathroom and
laundry) on a dimmer to soften harsh light.

~ 48 ~

Hang a hammock in the yard or on the deck.

~ 49 ~

Screen as many windows as possible so that, weather
permitting, you can bring the outdoors in.

~ 50 ~

Dry your sheets in the sun.

13

House Symbolism, Superstitions, and Folklore

A WINDOW, OR "WIND EYE," was originally a hole in the wall that opened the darkness to the holy power of light. Some ancient communities worshipped the first ray of light to reach a window.

A witch ball, or colorful glass sphere, could be hung in a window to distract the evil eye of a descending witch and absorb the first hit of her venom.

In many cultures, the threshold is mystical and sacred. People of these cultures avoid any contact between the foot and the threshold.

People used to believe witches rode broomsticks because they were afraid of horses. Nailing a horseshoe over the doorway kept witches from entering the home.

In parts of North Africa, animal genitalia are hung above barn doorways as a warning to passing demons.

Dream symbolism interprets the rooms of a house as different layers of the psyche. The roof rep-

resents the mind, the subconscious is rele-
gated to the basement, the hearth is the
heart, the threshold free will.

Foundations of houses in Old World
Europe were laid in blood, a sacrificial rite
intended to calm the earth deity and ensure
architectural stability.

It's still a common practice in northern Europe and
America to carry bread and salt into a new house to
ensure prosperity for the occupants.

In Ireland a cup of milk is placed on the windowsill
as refreshment for the wandering family ghosts who pass
by at Christmastime.

In parts of Europe and North America, the belief still
prevails that a newly completed house should be placed
under the protection of a lucky tree.

In Europe the houseleek plant is sometimes grown
upon roofs to thwart attacks of hostile spirits.

The keyhole represents a home's entry point for dev-
ils. Many people once believed that stopping the keyhole
was important during childbirth to keep the fairies from
stealing the baby.

The oak is the sacred tree of the thunder god, protecting homes against thunder and lightning. This is why bobbins on window cords are acorn-shaped.

Bees bring great luck and domestic harmony to a house. So does a common house spider. "If you wish to live and thrive, let a spider run alive," is a friendly maxim for the superstitious home dweller.

An Early American tradition that dates back to the Druids is to hang a sapling at the highest point in a house or barn under construction. Traditionally done at the end of a house or barn raising, this act was intended to apologize to all the trees that were killed to build the structure and to symbolize the birth of new life.

Before cars were invented, travelers commonly sliced a small sliver from the lintel of their front door and carried it with them on their journey. The ritual was thought to ensure that the trip would be safe and the house would still be standing when the traveler returned home.

Acknowledgments

I AM GRATEFUL TO ALL the people who shared their knowledge and enthusiasm with me as I wrote this book: Charlie Schiffman, Jen Feldman, Rabbi Geller, Karen Sheppard, Father Demetri Tsigas, Candace Schefe and the staff and volunteers at Holy Trinity Church in Portland, Oregon, Marie Clohessy, Neal Hatayama and the Hawaii State Public Library System, Dr. Sagi Naya, Eric Marcoux, Marcelino Ugaldi, the University of Nevada Basque Studies Program, Robert M. Villigas, the Rev. Nobuharu Uzunoe, Jerre Grimm, Christa Grimm, Dr. Richard Townsend.

Bibliography

Attwater, Donald. *The Penguin Dictionary of Saints.*
London, Eng.: Penguin Books, 1965.

Benedict, Ruth. *Zuni Mythology,* 2 vols. New York:
Columbia University Press, 1935.

Julienne Bennett and Mimi Luebbermann. *Where the
Heart Is: A Celebration of Home.* Berkeley, Calif.:
Wildcat Canyon Press, 1995.

Cavendish, Marshall. *Man, Myth & Magic: The
Illustrated Encyclopedia of Mythology, Religion and the
Unknown.* New York: Marsh Cavendish Corp., 1985.

Coniaris, Anthony M. *Making God Real in the Orthodox Christian Home.* Minneapolis: Light and Life Publishing Co., 1977.

Covarrubias, Miguel. *Island of Bali.* New York: Knopf, 1956.

Cushing, Frank Hamilton. *Selected Writings: Zuni.* Lincoln: University of Nebraska Press, 1979.

Eggan, Fred. *Social Organization of the Western Pueblos.* Chicago: University of Chicago Press, 1950.

Eiseman, Fred B., Jr. *Bali and Lombok.* New York: Prentice Hall Travel, 1993.

Fairon, Pat. *Irish Blessings: Irish Prayers and Blessings for All Occasions.* San Francisco: Chronicle Books, 1992.

Frisbie, Charlotte Johnson. *Navajo Medicine Bundles or "Jish": Acquisition, Transmission, and Disposition in the Past and Present.* Albuquerque: University of New Mexico Press, 1987.

Gallop, Rodney. *A Book of the Basques.* London: Macmillan and Co., Ltd., 1930.

Greenburg, Blu. *How to Run a Traditional Jewish Household.* New York: Simon & Schuster, Inc., 1983.

Grimes, Joel. *Navajo: Portrait of a Nation.* Englewood, Colo.: Westcliffe Publishers, Inc., 1992.

Gross, David C. *The Jewish People's Almanac.* New York: Hippocrene Books, Inc., 1988.

Habitat for Humanity, International. Dedication Prayer, Americas, GA.

Handy, E. S. Craighill, et al. *Ancient Hawaiian Civilizations.* Vt.: Charles E. Tuttle Co., Inc., 1965.

Humez, Jean M. *Mother's First Born Daughters: Early Shaker Writings on Women and Religion.* Bloomington: Indiana University Press, 1993.

Walter Krickenberg, Hermann Trimborn, Werner Muller, and Otto Zerries. *Pre-Columbian*

American Religions. New York: Holt, Rinehart & Winston, 1969.

Lip, Evelyn. *Feng Shui in the Home.* Torrance, Calif.: Heian Publishers, 1991.

National Conference of Catholic Bishops. *Catholic Household Blessings and Prayers.* Washington, D.C.: U.S. Catholic Conference, 1989.

O'Faolain, Sean. *The Irish: A Character Study.* New York: Devin-Adair, 1949.

Ott, Sandra. *The Circle of Mountains: A Basque Shepherding Community.* Reno: University of Nevada Press, 1981.

Parsons, Elsie C. *Pueblo Indian Religion.* Chicago: University of Chicago Press, 1939.

Powell, J. W. *The 17th Annual Report of the Bureau of American Ethnography, Vol. 2.* Washington, D.C.: U.S. Government Printing Office, 1898.

Reichard, Gladys A. *Navaho Religion: A Study of Symbolism.* Princeton, N.J.: Princeton University Press, 1977.

Rossback, Sarah. *Feng Shui: The Chinese Art of Placement.* New York: E. P. Dutton, 1983.

Ryan, M. J. *A Grateful Heart.* Berkeley, Calif.: Conari Press, 1994.

Sprigs, June. *By Shaker Hands.* New York: Alfred A. Knopf, 1975.

Vogt, Evon Z., and Ethel M. Albert, eds. *People of Rimrock: A Study of Values in Five Cultures.* Cambridge: Harvard University Press, 1966.

About the Author

ANN WALL FRANK is a freelance writer and world traveler. She wrote a shelter feature called Homing Instincts for the *Portland Oregonian* for five years. She has written about houses designed by Shakers, houses designed and furnished according to the principles of *feng shui*, brightly painted Victorians, log cabins, neo-Gothic mansions, humble bungalows, and houseboats. She has built two homes, remodeled two homes, and blessed twelve homes, apartments, and gardens. She is a student of *feng shui*. She is the author of a funny cookbook of comfort-food recipes, *Cooking for Your Evil Twin (Plume)*. Frank lives in Portland, Oregon, with her husband.